GW00384458

An anniversary edition
of the first
FOUR TALES
from
HANS ANDERSEN

Illustrated with woodcuts
by **Gwen Raverat**

Cambridge University Press
Cambridge
London   New York   New Rochelle
Melbourne   Sydney

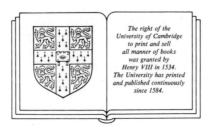

The right of the University of Cambridge to print and sell all manner of books was granted by Henry VIII in 1534. The University has printed and published continuously since 1584.

Published by the Press Syndicate of the University of Cambridge
The Pitt Building, Trumpington Street, Cambridge CB2 1RP
32 East 57th Street, New York, NY 10022, USA
10 Stamford Road, Oakleigh, Melbourne 3166, Australia

First published 1935
Anniversary Edition 1986

Printed in Great Britain at the University Press, Cambridge

British Library cataloguing in publication data
Andersen, H.C.
An anniversary edition of the first Four tales from
Hans Andersen.
I. Title II. Raverat, Gwen
839.8′136 [J]   PZ7

Library of Congress cataloging in publication data
Andersen, H. C. (Hans Christian), 1805–1875.
An anniversary edition of the first four tales from
Hans Andersen.
   Summary: The four illustrated selections include
"The Tinder Box," "Little Claus and Big Claus,"
"The Princess and the Pea," and "Little Ida's Flowers."
   1. Fairy tales – Denmark. 2. Children's stories, Danish.
[1. Fairy tales] I. Raverat, Gwen, 1885–1957, ill. II. Title.
III. Title: Four tales from Hans Andersen.
PZ8.A54   1986b [Fic]   86–13665

ISBN 0 521 33069 6

FOUR TALES FROM
HANS ANDERSEN

FOUR TALES
from
HANS ANDERSEN

A New Version of the First Four

by

R. P. KEIGWIN

Illustrated with woodcuts by
GWEN RAVERAT

CAMBRIDGE
at the University Press
1935

CONTENTS

INTRODUCTION

Looking back a hundred years and bearing in mind the number of *Eventyr* that Andersen wrote, one is astonished to see how representative this original instalment turns out to be and how surely the poet jumped at once into his stride. "I have started"—he wrote to Ingemann early in 1835—"on one or two tales, told for children, and I fancy I have been successful."

The stories he re-tells are some of those which he used to enjoy hearing in his childhood on the island of Fyn, but each of the four has a clearly-

marked style of its own. In *The Tinder-Box*—
where the Soldier is plainly Andersen himself,
cock-a-hoop at the impending success of his
first novel—the tone is jaunty, devil-may-
care; in *Little Claus and Big Claus*, that
hilarious folk-farce, his naïveté is given full
rein, but the effect is always sturdy and
stimulating. Money is really the main theme
of both these stories—and money was what the
needy Andersen most desired at the moment.
Perhaps a "princess" should be added to his
wants at that time; hence *The Princess and the
Pea*, where there is a characteristic vein of
irony which makes the diminutive tale itself
a kind of test for sensibility. Finally, in *Little
Ida's Flowers*, a dream-tale as gentle and fragile
as the blooms that people it, quite another sort
of Andersen is revealed, with faint foreshadow-
ings of Lewis Carroll—Ida Thiele is his Alice
Liddell. *Little Ida* is indeed full of intimacies,
reminding us how parochial the Copenhagen of
that era was; and though the story comes partly
from Hoffmann, its treatment is quite original.
Here, too, Andersen summed up, unconsciously
enough, his ultimate experience of the opposite

sex: "So the chimney-sweep danced by himself, and he didn't get on at all badly either."

A word must be added about Andersen's diction, because it was this, above all, which incurred the wrath of his early critics and was yet in the end to exert a powerful influence on the future of Danish prose. "I have written them down"—he said of his *Eventyr* in that same letter to Ingemann—"just as I would tell them to a child." That is to say, he abandoned the so-called literary style in favour of the natural, conversational forms of speech. "The style" (he wrote in later years) "should enable one to hear the voice of the person who is telling the story, and the language should therefore lend itself to the spoken word." It sounds like a treatise on Broadcast English; and indeed Andersen was, in a sense, the original broadcaster. He did actually, by nearly a hundred years, anticipate that simplified technique of language which is said to be one of the major missions of the B.B.C.

He sprinkled his narrative with every kind of conversational touch—crisp, lively openings, to catch the listener's attention at a swoop;

frequent asides or parentheses; little bits of Copenhagen slang; much grammatical licence; and, above all, a free use of particles—those nods and nudges of speech, with which Danish (like Greek) is so richly endowed. So completely did Andersen maintain the conversational tone in his *Tales* that you are quite shocked when you occasionally come across some really literary turn. Furthermore, he says "the tales are told for children, but older people should be able to listen". The language is therefore not limited to children's language, but to language which children can understand and enjoy. (It is extraordinary, by the way, how far removed Andersen's language is from that found in Grimm—to say nothing of his humour, which is for Danes his best-loved feature. The common impression, in England, of his being sentimental is also largely erroneous.)

So much, in brief compass, for Andersen's technique of language, often alas! obscured by a translator's desire to embellish and, in fact, give to the author's prose just those qualities which are triumphantly absent from the original. For the rest, here are his first four stories, very well able to speak for themselves, even though one may despair of ever transferring the true Danish flavour into the English text. Andersen, who was the discoverer of the child in Denmark, is the benefactor of the child in almost every country and every language. Happy indeed—as a Frenchman wrote not so long ago—happy are those who, in the belief that they are writing for children, have appealed to humanity at large, for they are the kings of the earth.

THE TINDER-BOX

THE TINDER-BOX

L eft, right! Left, right!...Down the country-road came a soldier marching. Left, right! Left, right!...He had his knapsack on his back and a sword at his side, for he had been at the war, and now he was on his way home. But then he met an old witch on the road. Oh! she was ugly—her lower lip hung right down on her chest. "Good evening, soldier," she said, "what a nice sword you've got, and what a big knapsack! You're a proper soldier! Now I'll show you how to get as much money as you want!" "Thank you very much, old dame!" said the soldier.

"Do you see that big tree over there?" said the witch, pointing to a tree near by. "It's quite hollow inside. Now, you must climb

right up it, and then you'll see a hole; slip through this, and you'll come deep down into the tree. I will tie a rope round your waist, so that I can haul you up again, as soon as you give me a shout."

3

"But what am I to do down in the tree?" asked the soldier.

"Fetch money!" answered the witch. "For, mind you, when you get down to the bottom of the tree, you will find yourself in a large passage. It's quite light there, because hundreds of lamps are burning there. Next, you will see three doors; you can open them all right, for the key's in the lock. If you go into the first room, you will see in the middle of the floor a big chest, with a dog sitting on it which has got eyes as big as tea-cups; but never you mind about that! I'll give you my blue-check apron, and you can spread it out on the floor. Then go along quickly and lift off the dog and put it on my apron; open the lid of the chest, and take just as many pennies as you like. They are all copper, but if you would rather have silver, then you must go into the next room. There sits a dog with eyes as large as mill-wheels, but never you mind about that! Put the dog down on my apron, and help yourself to the money! And yet, if it's gold you want, you can get that too—as much as ever you can carry— if only you go into the third room. But this

4

time the dog which is sitting on the money-chest has two eyes each one as big as the Round Tower....Something like a dog, I can tell you! But never you mind a bit about that! Just put the dog down on my apron, and then it won't do you any harm, and you can take as much gold out of the chest as you like."

"That doesn't sound at all bad", said the soldier. "But tell me, old witch, what am I to give you? Because I expect you'll be wanting your share!"

"No," said the witch, "not a single penny will I take. You've simply got to bring me an old tinder-box, which my grandmother forgot, when she was last down there."

"Oh, come on, then! let me get that rope round my middle!" said the soldier.

"Here it is," said the witch, "and here's my blue-check apron."

Then the soldier crawled up the tree, let himself down, plump! through the hole, and now he was standing, as the witch had said, down in the great passage where the hundreds of lamps were burning.

Then he unlocked the first door. Ugh! there

sat the dog with eyes as big as tea-cups and glared at him.

"You're a nice chap, you are!" said the soldier. He put it down on the witch's apron and took just as many copper pennies as he could stuff into his pocket. Then he shut the chest, put the dog up again and went into the

second room. Bless my soul! there sat the dog with eyes as big as mill-wheels.

"You shouldn't stare at me so!" said the soldier; "you'll strain your eyes." And then he put the dog down on the witch's apron; but when he saw such piles of silver in the chest, he threw away all the coppers he had got and filled up his pockets and his knapsack with nothing but silver. And now he went into the

third room!...Oh, but it was horrible! The dog in there had actually got two great eyes as big as the Round Tower, and they were going round and round in its head like wheels!

"Good evening!" said the soldier; and he touched his cap, because never in his life had he seen such a dog. But after he had looked at it for a bit, he thought to himself, "Enough of that!" and went and lifted the dog down on to

7

the floor and opened the chest—why, goodness gracious, what a lot of gold there was! There was enough for him to buy the whole of Copenhagen, all the sugar-pigs that the cake-women sell, and all the tin-soldiers and whips and rocking-horses in the world. Yes, yes, plenty of money in there—my word, there was!

So at once the soldier emptied out all the silver coins from his pockets and his knapsack and put in gold instead; yes, and he filled up everything with gold, his pockets, his knapsack, his cap and even his boots, so that he could hardly walk. Now he had got some money! He put the dog back on the chest, slammed the door, and then shouted up through the tree, "Hi, mother! haul me up again, will you?"

"Have you got the tinder-box?" asked the witch.

"Oh no! that's true, I had clean forgotten it", said the soldier; and he went straight back and fetched it. The witch hauled him up out of the tree, and there he was again, standing on the road with his pockets, boots, cap and knapsack bulging with money.

8

"What are you going to do with this tinder-box?" asked the soldier.

"That's no business of yours!" answered the witch. "You've got your money; now just give me my tinder-box!"

"Rubbish!" said the soldier. "Tell me at once what you want to do with it—or I'll have out my sword and cut your head off."

"No", said the witch.

So he cut off her head....There she lay!

But the soldier tied up all his money in her apron and made a bundle of it, to go on his back. He put the tinder-box in his pocket and went straight on into the town.

It was a fine town, and he put up at the finest inn. He ordered the very best rooms and the food he was most fond of; for, now that he had all that money, he was a rich man. The servant who had to clean his boots thought, well, this was a funny old pair of boots for such a rich gentleman to have; but he hadn't yet bought any new ones. The next day he went out and got some good boots and some really smart clothes. And now the soldier had become quite a fashionable gentleman, and they told him all about the sights of their town, and about their King, and what a pretty Princess his daughter was.

"Where is she to be seen?" asked the soldier.

"She just isn't to be seen", they all answered. "She lives in a big copper castle with lots of walls and towers all round it. No one but the king is allowed to go to her there, because a fortune-teller once said that she is to marry a common soldier, and the king doesn't like that at all."

"My word! I should like to see her", thought the soldier; but of course he couldn't possibly get leave to.

And now he lived a merry life.

He was always going to the theatre, or driving in the Park; and he gave away lots of money to the poor. That was very nice of him; you see, he remembered so well from the old days how awful it was to be absolutely penniless. But now he was rich and well-dressed, and so he made lots of friends who all said what a fine fellow he was—a real gentleman—and the soldier liked that very much. But as he was

10

spending money every day and never getting any back, at last he had only got twopence left; and so he had to move from the fine rooms he had been living in and go and live in a little poky attic right under the roof. He had to clean his own boots and mend them with a darning-needle, and none of his friends ever came to see him, for there were such a lot of stairs to climb.

One evening, when it was quite dark and he couldn't even buy himself a candle, he suddenly remembered that there was a little bit of candle left in the tinder-box that he had got for the old witch out of the hollow tree. So he fetched out the tinder-box and the bit of candle; but just as he was striking a light and the sparks flew up from the flint, the door sprang open, and the dog he had seen down in the tree with eyes as big as tea-cups stood before him and said "What are my lord's commands?"

"I say!" said the soldier. "This must be a rum sort of tinder-box, if I can get whatever I want like that." "Bring me some money", he said to the dog; then flick! and away it

11

went, and flick! here it was back again, with a
large bagful of pennies in its mouth.

And now the soldier realised what a splendid
tinder-box it was. One stroke brought before
him the dog which sat on the chest with the
copper money; two strokes, the dog with the
silver; and three strokes, the dog with the
gold. The soldier lost no time in changing back
into the fine rooms and the smart clothes, and
of course all his friends remembered him again
at once and were tremendously fond of
him.

And then one day he thought to himself
"There's something queer about this, that no
one's allowed to see the Princess. She's sup-
posed to be so very lovely, according to all
these people; but what's the good of that, if
she has to sit the whole time inside the copper
castle, the one that has all those towers?
Can't I possibly manage to see her somehow?
Now then, where's my tinder-box?" So he
struck a light and flick! there stood the dog
with the eyes as big as tea-cups.

"Of course I know it's the middle of the
night," said the soldier, "but all the same I

would like to see the Princess, that I would!
Just for half a jiffy!"

The dog was out of the door in a flash and,
before the soldier had time to think about it,
there was the dog
again with the Prin-
cess lying asleep on
his back; and she
looked so lovely
that anyone could
see she was a real
princess; and the
soldier simply
couldn't resist, he
had to kiss her—
he was a soldier all
over.

Then the dog
scuttled back again
with the Princess; but in the morning, when
the King and Queen were at breakfast, the
Princess said she had had such a curious dream
in the night, about a dog and a soldier. She had
ridden on the dog's back, and the soldier had
kissed her.

13

"That's a pretty tale, if you like!" said the Queen.

And so one of the old ladies-in-waiting was told to sit up the following night by the Princess's bed and see if it was really a dream or not.

The soldier did so long for another look at the pretty Princess; and so up came the dog

by night and took her and dashed off at full speed. But the old lady-in-waiting put on her overboots and ran just as fast after them, and when she saw them disappear into a big house she thought to herself, "Now I know where it is", and chalked up a big cross on the door. Then she went home to bed, and the dog came back too with the Princess. But when it saw a cross had been chalked on the door where

14

the soldier was living, the dog also took a bit of chalk and put a cross on every door in the town. That was a clever idea, because now, you see, the lady-in-waiting couldn't find the right door, as there were crosses on the whole lot of them.

Early in the morning the King and Queen, the old lady-in-waiting and all the Court officials sallied forth in order to see where it was the Princess had been.

"Here's the house!" said the King, when he saw the first door with a cross on it.

"No, it's there, darling!" said the Queen, catching sight of the second door with a cross on it.

"But here's another—and there's another!" they all kept saying. Whichever way they turned, there were crosses on the doors. So then they soon realised that it was no good searching any longer.

But the Queen, you know, was a very clever

15

woman, who could do more than just drive out in a coach. She took her great golden scissors and cut up a large piece of silk and sewed the pieces together into a pretty little bag, which she filled with the finest buckwheat flour. She fastened the little bag to the Princess's back, and then she snipped a little hole in the bag, so as to sprinkle the flour wherever the Princess went.

At night, up came the dog once more, took the Princess on his back and ran off with her to the soldier, who loved her so dearly and did so wish he were a prince and could marry her.

The dog never noticed how the flour kept leaking out all the way from the castle to the soldier's window, where it ran up the wall with the Princess. The next morning it was quite plain to the King and Queen where their daughter had been going; so they took the soldier and put him in prison.

There he sat. Ugh! how dark and dreary his cell was! And, besides, they kept saying to him "To-morrow you're going to be hanged!" That didn't sound at all cheerful, and the worst of it was he had left his tinder-box at the

16

inn. In the morning, through the iron bars of his little window, he watched people hurrying out of the town to see him hanged. He heard the drums and saw the soldiers marching past. Everyone was afoot. Among them was a

cobbler's boy in leather apron and slippers; he was trotting along so fast that one of his slippers came off and flew right against the wall where the soldier sat peeping out between the iron bars.

"I say! you young cobbler, you don't need to hurry like that," the soldier said to him, "they can't begin without me. But look here —if you will kindly run along to where I've been living and fetch me my tinder-box, you shall have twopence for your trouble; but mind you get a move on!" The cobbler's boy was very glad to earn twopence, so he sprinted off for the tinder-box, brought it to the soldier, and—well, now listen to what happened!

Outside the town a high gallows had been built, and round about it stood the soldiers and thousands and thousands of people. The King and Queen sat on a beautiful throne opposite the judge and all his councillors.

Already the soldier had climbed the ladder; but just as they were going to put the rope round his neck he reminded them that, before being executed, a criminal always had the right to ask for one harmless favour. He said he would so like to smoke a pipe of tobacco— after all, it would be the last pipe he could smoke in this world.

Now, the King didn't like to say no to that; so the soldier took his tinder-box and struck a light—one, two, three!—and there stood all three dogs: the one with eyes as big as tea-cups, the one with eyes like mill-wheels, and the one which had eyes as big as the Round Tower.

"Save me now from being hanged!" said the soldier; and then the dogs flew at the judges and all the councillors, and seized some by their legs and others by their noses, and tossed them so high into the air that when they came down they were dashed to pieces.

18

"I won't be tossed!" said the King; but the biggest dog picked them both up, King and Queen, and sent them hurtling after the others. Then the soldiers got frightened, and the people all shouted out "Soldier boy, you shall be our King and have the pretty Princess". And they put the soldier into the King's coach, and all three dogs went dancing in front of it and cried out "Hurrah!" And the boys whistled on their fingers, and the soldiers presented arms. The Princess came out of the copper castle and was made Queen, and how pleased she was! The wedding-feast lasted for a week, and the dogs sat at table with everyone else and kept rolling their great big eyes.

LITTLE CLAUS AND BIG CLAUS

LITTLE CLAUS AND
BIG CLAUS

There were two men in one village, who both had the very same name; they were both called Claus. One of them owned four horses, the other only one; and, to tell them from each other, people called the man who had four horses Big Claus, and the man who had only one horse Little Claus. Now let us hear how these two got on; for this is a true story.

All through the week Little Claus had to plough for Big Claus and lend him his one horse; in return, Big Claus gave him the help

22

of all his four horses, but only once a week, and
that was on Sunday. My word! How Little
Claus did crack his whip over all five horses!
They were as good as his—for that one day.
The sun shone so pleasantly, and the church-
bells were all ringing for church; the villagers
went by in their Sunday best, with their
hymn-books under their arms, to hear the
parson preach, and when they looked at Little
Claus ploughing with five horses, he was so
delighted that he cracked his whip once more
and cried out: "Gee up, all my horses!"

"You mustn't say that," said Big Claus;
"there's only one horse, you know, which is
yours." But when some more people went
past on their way to church, Little Claus forgot that he wasn't to say that and cried out
again: "Gee up, all my horses!"

"Look here, will you kindly give over?" said Big Claus. "The next time you say that, I'll give your horse a clump on the head and kill him on the spot; and that'll be good-bye to him."

"I promise you I won't say it again", said Little Claus. But when some more people went by and they nodded good-morning to him, he was so delighted and felt that it must look so smart for him to have five horses to plough his field with, that he cracked his whip and cried out: "Gee up, all my horses!"

"I'll gee up your horses for you!" said Big Claus, and he took the mallet for the tether-peg, and gave Little Claus's one horse such a clump on the forehead that it fell down stone dead.

"Oh, dear! Now I haven't a horse at all", said Little Claus and began to cry. By and by he flayed the dead horse and took the hide and gave it a thorough drying in the wind. Then he stuck it in a bag, which he threw over his shoulder, and went off to the next town to sell his horse-hide.

He had a long way to go, and it led through a

big, gloomy wood. Presently a terrible storm got up, and he quite lost his way. It was evening before he could find it again, and he was much too far from the town or from home to be able to reach either before night fell.

Close to the road stood a large farmhouse; the windows had the shutters up outside, but

yet a gleam of light showed over the top of them. "I daresay I can get leave to spend the night there", thought Little Claus and went up and knocked at the door.

The farmer's wife came and opened it; but when she heard what he wanted, she told him to be off, as her husband was not at home, and she didn't take in strangers.

"Oh, well, in that case I must find a bed out

of doors", said Little Claus, and the farmer's wife shut the door in his face.

Near by was a big haystack, and between this and the house a little shed had been built, with a flat thatch roof to it.

"I can sleep up there", said Little Claus, catching sight of the roof; "that will be a lovely bed, and I shouldn't think the stork will fly down and bite my legs"; for a real live stork was standing up there on the roof, where it had its nest.

Little Claus now crawled up on to the shed, where he lay and wriggled himself to get really comfortable. The wooden shutters didn't quite cover the windows up at the top, and so he was able to see right into the room.

There was a large table laid with wine and roast meat and oh! such a delicious-looking fish. The farmer's wife and the parish clerk were sitting at table all by themselves; and she kept filling up his glass for him, and he kept helping himself to the fish—he was very fond of fish.

"If only I could get a taste of that!" thought Little Claus, craning out his neck towards the

window. Heavens! What a gorgeous cake he could see in there! It was really a wonderful spread.

Then he heard someone riding along the road towards the house. It was the farmer himself, coming home.

Now, although he was an excellent man, the farmer had the strange failing that he never could bear the sight of a parish clerk; if he ever set eyes on a clerk, he flew into an absolute rage. And that was just why this clerk had called in to pass the time of day with the farmer's wife, when he knew that her husband was away from home; and the good woman set before him all the nicest things to eat that she could find. And now, when they heard the husband coming, they got so scared that the woman begged the clerk to creep into a big empty chest which stood over in the corner. So he climbed in, for he knew quite well that the poor man couldn't bear the sight of a parish clerk. The woman quickly hid away all the delicious food and wine inside her oven, because if her husband had seen it he would have been sure to ask what it all meant.

28

"Oh, dear!" sighed Little Claus up on the shed, when he saw all the food disappearing.

"Is that somebody up there?" asked the farmer, peering up at Little Claus. "What are you lying up there for? Much better come along o' me into the house!"

Little Claus then explained how he had lost his way and asked if he might stop the night.

"Why, certainly," said the farmer, "but first we must have a bit o' something to eat."

The farmer's wife gave them both a most friendly welcome, laid a long table and gave them a large bowl of porridge. The farmer was hungry, and he ate with a good appetite; but Little Claus couldn't help thinking about the lovely roast meat, the fish and the cake which he knew were inside the oven.

Under the table, at his feet, he had placed his sack with the horse-hide in it; for we mustn't forget, it was the hide which he had brought away with him from home, in order to sell it in the town. He didn't care for the porridge at all; and so he trod on his bag, and the dry hide inside it gave out quite a loud squeak.

29

"''Sh!" said Little Claus to his sack; but at the same time he trod on it again, and it gave out a still louder squeak.

"Why, what ever have you got in that there bag?" asked the farmer.

"Oh, it's a wizard", said Little Claus. "He says that we shouldn't be eating porridge; he has conjured the whole oven full of meat and fish and cake."

"You don't say so!" said the farmer, and in a twinkling he opened the oven and saw all the delicious food which his wife had hidden away, though he thought himself that the wizard had conjured it there. His wife didn't dare say a word; she put the food straight on the table, and they both made a good meal off the fish and the meat and the cake. Presently Little Claus trod on his bag once more and made the hide squeak.

"What's he say now?" asked the farmer.

"He says", answered Little Claus, "that he has also conjured us three bottles of wine, and they're in the oven too." So the wife had to bring out the wine she had hidden, and the farmer drank and became quite merry; he felt

he'd give anything to own a wizard like the one
Little Claus had got in his bag.

"Can he also make the devil appear?" asked
the farmer. "I should so like to see him, now
that I'm feeling so cheerful."

"Certainly," said Little Claus, "my wizard
can do whatever I like to ask him—can't you,
old man?" and at the same time he trod on the
bag so that it squeaked. "Did you hear him?
He says, yes, of course he can; but the devil's
so hideous, that you'd better not see him."

"Oh, I'm not afeard. What d'you think
he'll look like?"

"Well, you'll find he's the very image of a
parish clerk."

"Lumme!" said the farmer, "that's hideous
and no mistake! You know, I can't abear the
sight of parish clerks; but never mind, I know
it's the devil this time, so I reckon I'll put up
with it for once. I'm full o' pluck just now—
but don't let him come too near!"

"Now I'll ask my wizard", said Little Claus,
treading on the bag and turning his ear to it.

"What's he say?"

"He says you may go up and open the chest

which is standing over there in the corner, and you'll see the devil squatting inside; but mind you hold on to the lid, or he'll slip out."

"Come and help me hold it, then!" said the farmer, going across to the chest in which his

wife had hidden the real clerk, who sat there trembling with fear.

The farmer raised the lid a little way and peeped in under it: "Lumme!" he shrieked and jumped back from the chest. "Yes, I saw him right enough; he looked the dead spit of our clerk—oh, it was horrible!"

They had to have a drink after that, and they went on drinking far into the night.

"You must sell me that wizard", said the farmer. "Ask what you like for him! I tell you what, I'll give you a whole bushel of money straight away."

"No", said Claus. "I can't do that. Just think of the profit I can make out of this wizard."

"Oh, but I'm fair crazy to have him", said the farmer, and he begged and pleaded till at last Little Claus said yes. "You've been very kind and given me a good night's lodging, so it doesn't make much odds. You shall have the wizard for a bushel of money, but full measure, mind you!"

"Right you are!" said the farmer. "But you must take that there chest with you; I won't have it another hour in the place—he may be in there yet, for all we can tell."

Little Claus gave the farmer his sack with the dry hide in it, and got a whole bushel of money, full measure, in exchange. What's more, the farmer gave him a large barrow on which to wheel away the chest and the money.

"Good-bye!" said Little Claus, and off he

K   33   5

went trundling his money and the great chest with the clerk still in it.

On the other side of the wood ran a deep river, where the current was so strong that you could hardly swim against it. A big bridge had lately been built across it, and Little Claus halted when he got to the middle and said out aloud, so that the clerk in the chest could hear him: "Hang it all! What ever am I to do with this stupid chest? It's so heavy, you'd think it was full of stones. I'm sick and tired of wheeling it, so I'll just tip it into the river. Then, if it sails home to me, very good; and if it doesn't—well, it can't be helped."

Then he took hold of the chest by one of the handles and tilted it a bit, as though he meant to hurl it down into the water.

"Stop! Stop!" shouted the clerk from inside the chest. "Let me out! Oh, do let me out!"

"Good gracious!" said Little Claus and pretended to be frightened. "He's still inside! I must push him into the river at once, and then he'll drown!"

"No! No!" shouted the clerk. "I'll give you a whole bushel of money, if you'll let me out."

"Ah, that's another story", said Little Claus and opened the chest. The clerk quickly crept out, pushed the empty chest into the water and went to his home, where Little Claus was given a whole bushel of money. He had already got one out of the farmer, so there he was now with his wheelbarrow chock-full of money.

"There! I got rather a good price for that horse!" he said to himself, when he came home to his own room and turned out all the money in a big heap on the floor. "Big Claus will be very annoyed when he hears how rich I've become out of my one horse; but all the same I won't tell him straight away."

Presently he sent a boy along to Big Claus to borrow a bushel measure.

"I wonder what he wants that for?" thought Big Claus, and he smeared the bottom with tar, so that a little of whatever was measured might stick to it; and, sure enough, when the measure came back, there were three new silver florins sticking to it.

"Hullo, what's this?" said Big Claus, and ran straight off to Little Claus. "Where did you get all this money from?"

35

"Oh, that was for my horse-hide that I sold yesterday."

"That's a wonderful good price!" said Big Claus; and he ran home, took an axe and gave all his four horses a clump on the forehead. Then he stripped off the hides and trundled them away into the town.

"Hides! Hides! Who'll buy my hides?" he shouted through the streets.

All the shoemakers and tanners came running up and asking how much he wanted for them.

"A bushel of money apiece!" said Big Claus.

"Are you mad?" they all asked him. "Do you suppose we keep money in bushels?"

"Hides! Hides! Who'll buy my hides?" he shouted again; but to everyone who asked him the price he answered: "A bushel of money."

"He's trying to make fools of us", they all said; and then the shoemakers took their straps and the tanners their leather aprons and began to give Big Claus a good beating.

"Hides! Hides!" they mocked at him, "we'll give you a hide that'll bleed like a pig! Out of the town with him!" they shouted; and

Big Claus had to bolt for his life—he'd never had such a drubbing.

"All right!" he said, when he got home. "Little Claus shall pay for this. I'll beat his brains out."

But at Little Claus's home his old grandmother had just died. It's true she had always

been very cross and unkind to him; still, he was very much grieved and took the dead woman and laid her in his own warm bed, to see if he couldn't bring her to life again. She was to lie there all night, while he himself would sit over in the corner and sleep on a chair; it wouldn't be the first time he had done that.

37

During the night, as he was sitting there, the door opened and Big Claus came in with an axe. He knew quite well where Little Claus's bed was, so he went straight up to it, and, thinking the dead grandmother was Little Claus, gave her a great clump on the forehead.

"There now!" he said, "you're not going to make a fool of me again"; and he went back home.

"What a very wicked man!" said Little Claus to himself. "It's clear that he meant to kill me. Anyhow, it's a good thing for the old dame that she was dead already, otherwise he would have taken her life."

And now he dressed up the old grandmother in her Sunday clothes, borrowed a horse from his neighbour, harnessed it to the cart and set up the old grandmother in the back seat, so that she couldn't fall out when he drove faster, and away they bowled through the woods. By sunrise they were outside a large inn, where Little Claus drew up and went inside to get something to eat.

The landlord of the inn had plenty of money and was a very kind man too; but he was hot-

38

tempered, as if he were full of pepper and snuff.

"Good morning!" he said to Little Claus. "You're out early to-day in your best clothes."

"Yes," said Little Claus, "I'm off to town with my old grandmother. She's sitting out in the cart; I can't get her to come in here. Will you take her a large glass of honey-wine? But you must speak rather loud, for she's a bit deaf."

"Right you are!" said the landlord and poured out a large glass of honey-wine, which he took out with him to the dead grandmother who was propped up in the cart.

"Here's a glass of honey-wine from your son, lady", said the landlord. But the dead woman never said a word nor moved a muscle.

"Can't you hear?" cried the landlord at the top of his voice; "here's a glass of honey-wine from your son!"

Once more he shouted it out, and yet again after that; but as she never stirred, he lost his temper and threw the glass right into her face, so that the wine ran down over her nose and she toppled over backwards into the cart; for she was only propped up and not fastened in.

39

"Hi! What's this?" cried Little Claus, rushing out and seizing the landlord by the throat. "You've been and killed my grandmother! Just look, there's a big hole in her forehead!"

"Oh, dear! That's a bit of bad luck!" cried the landlord, wringing his hands. "That all comes of my hot temper. Dear, kind Little Claus, I'll give you a whole bushel of money and bury your grandmother as if she was my own, if only you'll not say a word. Otherwise they'll cut off my head, and that is so beastly!"

So Little Claus got a whole bushel of money, and the landlord buried his old grandmother as if she had been his own.

As soon as Little Claus got back home with all his money, he sent his boy along to Big Claus to ask if he'd lend him a bushel measure.

"Hullo, what's this?" said Big Claus. "Didn't I kill him? I really must see about this myself." And he went over to Little Claus with the measure.

"Why, where ever have you got all this money from?" he asked, and my goodness!

40

how he opened his eyes when he saw all the fresh money that had come in.

"It was my grandmother you killed, not me", said Little Claus. "It's she I've just sold and got a bushel of money for."

"That's a wonderful good price", said Big Claus and hurried home, took an axe and quickly killed his old grandmother. Then he placed her in the cart, drove into the town where the doctor lived, and asked if he wanted to buy a dead body.

"Whose is it and where did you get it?" asked the doctor.

"It's my old grandmother", said Big Claus. "I killed her to get a bushel of money."

"Good gracious!" said the doctor, "you don't know what you're saying. Don't go babbling like that, or you may lose your head!" And then he told him frankly what a dreadfully wicked thing he had done, and what a bad man he was, and that he ought to be punished. This made Big Claus so frightened that he rushed straight out of the surgery into the cart, whipped up the horses and made for home. But the doctor and the rest of them

thought he was mad, and so they left him to
drive where he liked.

"You shall pay for this!" said Big Claus,
once he was out on the high-road. "Yes, you

shall certainly pay for this, Little Claus!" And,
as soon as he got home, he took the biggest
sack he could find, went along to Little Claus
and said: "You've been and fooled me again!
First, I killed my horses, and then my old
grandmother. It was your fault both times,

42

but you shan't fool me any more!" And he caught hold of Little Claus by the waist, thrust him into the sack, slung him over his shoulder and called out to him: "Now I'm going to take you out and drown you!"

There was some distance to go before he came to the river, and Little Claus was no light weight to carry. The road went past the church; and the sound of the organ playing and the people singing was so beautiful that Big Claus put down his sack, with Little Claus inside it, near by the church door and thought it would be nice to go in and listen to a hymn first before he went any further. Little Claus couldn't possibly get out, and everybody was in church; so in he went.

"Oh, dear! Oh, dear!" sighed Little Claus inside the sack. He wriggled and wriggled, but he couldn't possibly manage to get the string unfastened. Just then an old cattle-drover came up. His hair was as white as chalk, and he leaned on a big stick, as he drove a whole herd of cows and bullocks in front of him; these ran up to the sack, in which Little Claus was sitting, and overturned it.

43

"Oh, dear!" sighed Little Claus, "I'm so young to go to heaven!"

"And poor me!" said the drover, "I'm so old and I can't get there!"

"Open the sack!" called out Little Claus. "Crawl in here instead of me, and you'll soon get to heaven!"

"Ah! I'd give anything for that," said the drover, and he unfastened the sack for Little Claus, who jumped out at once.

"You'll mind the cattle, won't you?" said the old man, as he crawled into the bag. Little Claus tied it up and went on his way with all the cows and bullocks.

Soon after, Big Claus came out of church and put the sack over his shoulder again. Sure enough, he noticed that it seemed lighter; for the old drover wasn't more than half the weight of Little Claus. "How light he's become! No doubt it's because I listened to a hymn." Then off he went to the river, which was a deep one, and threw the sack with the old drover inside it right out into the stream and shouted after him, thinking of course that it was Little Claus: "There now! You shan't fool me any more!"

44

Then he turned homeward, but when he came to the cross-roads he met Little Claus driving off with all his cattle.

"Hullo, what's this?" said Big Claus, "didn't I drown you?"

"Yes, you did", said Little Claus. "You threw me into the river barely half an hour ago."

"But where did you get all those fine cattle from?" asked Big Claus.

"They're sea-cattle", said Little Claus. "I must tell you the whole story; and, by the by, thank you so much for drowning me. I'm in luck's way now; I'm really rich, I can tell you!...

"I was very frightened, as I lay inside the sack with the wind whistling round my ears, when you threw me down off the bridge into the cold water. I sank straight to the bottom, but I didn't hurt myself, because down there grows the finest, softest grass. As I came down on this, the bag at once opened, and the most lovely girl dressed in pure white, with a green garland on her wet hair, took my hand and said: 'Is that you, Little Claus? Here are a few

45

cattle for you to go on with. About four miles further up the road there's another drove of them, which I'll make you a present of'....

"Then I could see that the river was a great high-road for the sea-people. Down there at the bottom they walked and drove straight out of the sea, and then right away inland to where the river rises. It was delightful down there— what with flowers and the freshest grass, and fishes swimming about in the water and darting past my ears as birds do in the air up here. What fine folk there were, and what cattle to be met with along the hedges and ditches!"

"But why have you come up to us again in such a hurry?" asked Big Claus. "I wouldn't have done that, if it was so beautiful down there."

"Ah, but that's just where I've been rather cunning", said Little Claus. "You remember I told you what the sea-maiden said—that about four miles further up the road (and by the road she means of course the river, as she can't go anywhere else) there's another drove of cattle waiting for me. Well, I know how the river keeps winding in and out; it would be a

46

very roundabout way, you know. So, if you can do it, it's much shorter to come up on land and drive straight across to the river again. You see, I save almost half the distance that way and get to my sea-cattle more quickly."

"Oh, what a lucky man you are!" said Big Claus. "Do you think I shall get some sea-cattle too, if I go down to the bottom of the river?"

"I should just think you would!" said Little Claus; "but I can't carry you as far as the river in the sack, you're too heavy. If you will go there yourself and then crawl into the bag, I'll throw you into the water with the greatest of pleasure."

"Thanks very much," said Big Claus, "but if I don't find any sea-cattle when I get down there, I'll give you such a beating, I can tell you!"

"Oh, no; don't be so cruel!" So they went off to the river. The cattle were thirsty and, when they saw the water, they trotted off as fast as they could so as to get down and have a drink.

"Look what a hurry they're in", said Little

47

Claus. "They're longing to get down to the bottom again."

"Yes, but help me first", said Big Claus, "or you'll get your beating!" And then he crawled into the big sack, which had been lying across the back of one of the herd. "Better put a stone in, or else I'm afraid I mayn't sink", said Big Claus.

"I expect you'll sink all right", said Little Claus. Still, he put a big stone in the sack, tied the string tight and then gave it a good push—plomp!—there was Big Claus out in the river, and he sank straight to the bottom.

"I'm afraid he won't find his cattle", said Little Claus—and drove off home with what he had.

THE PRINCESS AND THE PEA

THE PRINCESS AND
THE PEA

nce upon a time there was a
Prince, who wanted to have a
Princess of his own, but she
must be a proper Princess. So he
travelled all over the world in
order to find such a one, but
every time there was something wrong. There
were plenty of Princesses, but he could never

quite make out if they were *real* Princesses; there was always something that wasn't quite right. So he came back home and was very much upset, because he did so long for a real Princess.

One evening a terrible storm blew up. There was lightning and thunder, the rain came pouring down—it was something dreadful!

All at once there was a knock at the city gate, and the old King went out to open it.

It was a Princess standing outside. But goodness! what a sight she was with the rain and the weather! The water was running all down her hair and her clothes, and in at the tip of her shoes and out again at the heels; and yet she declared she was a real Princess.

"Well, we shall soon see about that!"

53

thought the old Queen. She didn't say anything, but she went into the bedroom, took off
all the bedclothes and placed a pea on the
bottom of the bed; then she took twenty
mattresses and laid them on top of the pea,
and then again twenty of the softest feather-
beds on top of the mattresses. That's where the
Princess had to sleep for the night.

In the morning they asked her how she had
slept. "Oh, dreadfully badly!" said the Princess. "I hardly had a wink of sleep all night!
Goodness knows what there was in the bed! I
was lying on something so hard that I'm
simply black and blue all over. It's perfectly
dreadful!"

So then of course they could see that she
really *was* a Princess, because she had felt the

54

pea right through the twenty mattresses and the twenty feather-beds. Nobody but a real Princess could have such a tender skin as that.

And so the Prince took her to wife, because now he knew that he had a proper Princess. And the pea was sent to the museum, where it is still to be seen, unless someone has taken it.

There, that's something like a story, isn't it?

LITTLE IDA'S FLOWERS

LITTLE IDA'S FLOWERS

y poor flowers are quite dead!" said little Ida. "Yesterday evening they were so pretty, and now their leaves are all drooping. Why is it?" she asked of the student who was sitting on the sofa. She was very fond of him, because he knew the most lovely stories and could cut out such amusing pictures—hearts with little dancing ladies inside them, flowers, and great castles with doors that opened. He was a very jolly student.

"Why do the flowers look so unwell to-day?" she asked once more, pointing to a whole nosegay that was quite withered.

58

"Ah! don't you know what's the matter with them?" said the student. "The flowers were at a dance last night, that's why they're hanging their heads."

"But flowers can't dance!" said little Ida.

"Can't they!" said the student. "When it's dark and we are all asleep, they go hopping

round quite gaily; almost every night in the year they have a dance."

"Are children allowed to join in?"

"Certainly", said the student; "tiny little daisies are allowed to, and lilies-of-the-valley."

"Where do the loveliest flowers dance?" asked little Ida.

"You've often been out of town, haven't you, to look at all the beautiful flowers in the

59

garden of the great castle where the King lives in summer? Then you must have seen the swans which swim up to you, when you offer them breadcrumbs. There are wonderful dances out there, I can tell you!"

"I was out in that garden yesterday with my mother", said Ida, "but the leaves were all off the trees, and there wasn't a single flower left. Where are they? I saw so many there last summer."

"They are inside the castle", said the student. "You see, directly the King and all his

Court come back to town, the flowers at once run up from the garden into the castle and make merry. You should just see them! The two finest roses go and sit on the throne—they are King and Queen. All the red cockscombs

line up on both sides and bow—they are gentlemen-in-waiting. Then come all the prettiest flowers, and there is a grand ball. The blue violets are young naval cadets, and they dance with the hyacinths and crocuses, whom they call Miss. The tulips and the large yellow lilies are old dowagers, who keep an

61

eye on the dancing and see that everybody behaves."

"But look here", asked little Ida, "isn't there anyone to scold the flowers for dancing at the King's castle?"

"Nobody really knows what's going on"; said the student. "Sometimes, it's true, the old castle-steward, who is on watch there, comes along at night with his great bunch of keys; but as soon as the flowers hear the keys rattle, they don't make a sound, but hide behind the long curtains and poke their heads out. 'I can smell flowers in here', says the old steward, but he can't see them."

"What fun!" said little Ida, clapping her hands. "But shouldn't I be able to see the flowers either?"

"Oh, yes!" said the student. "You must just remember, next time you go out there, to peep in at the windows. You'll be sure to see the flowers. I did to-day. I saw a long yellow daffodil lolling on the sofa and pretending she was a maid-of-honour."

"Can the flowers in the Botanical Garden go out there too? Can they go all that way?"

"Ra-ther!" said the student, "because they can fly, if they want to. You've seen lots of pretty butterflies, haven't you? Red ones and white ones and yellow ones—they almost look like flowers, don't they? They *were* flowers once, but then they jumped off their stalks high into the air and kept flapping their petals as if they were little wings, and away they flew. And as they behaved nicely, they got leave to fly about by day as well—they didn't have to go back and sit still on their stalks—and so at last their petals grew into real wings. You've seen that, of course, yourself. All the same, it's quite possible that the flowers at the Botanical Garden have never been out to the King's castle and that they have no idea of the fun that goes on there at night. Well, now I'm going to tell you something which will quite astonish the Professor of Botany who lives close by—you know him, don't you? When you go into his garden, you're to tell one of the flowers that there's a grand ball out at the castle. This flower will be sure to pass the news on to the others, and so they will all fly away. Then, if the Professor walks out into his

63

garden, there won't be a single flower left and he won't have the slightest idea what has become of them."

"But how can the flower tell the others about the ball? Flowers can't talk, can they?"

"No, not exactly", answered the student; "but they do it by signs. Surely you've noticed them, when it's a bit windy—how the flowers keep nodding and fluttering their green leaves; that means as much to them as if they talked."

"Does the Professor understand their signs, then?" asked Ida.

"I should just think he does! Why, one morning he went into his garden and saw a great stinging-nettle making signs with its leaves to a lovely red carnation; it was saying, 'You *are* so attractive, and I *am* so fond of you!' But the Professor can't bear that sort of thing, and he at once rapped the stinging-nettle over its leaves—for they are its fingers—but in doing this he stung himself and, ever since, he has always been afraid to touch a stinging-nettle."

"What fun!" said little Ida, with a laugh.

"Fancy filling a child's head with such rubbish!" said the grumpy old Councillor,

who had come to pay a visit and was sitting
on the sofa. He never could bear the student
and always got cross when he saw him cutting
out those comic figures which were so amusing
—sometimes it was a man hanging from a
gibbet, with a heart in his hand because he was
a stealer of hearts; sometimes an old witch
riding on a broomstick, with her
husband perch-
ed on the bridge
of her nose. The
Councillor couldn't
bear that sort of thing,
and he always used to
say just what he said
now: "What rubbish to put
into a child's head! All stuff
and nonsense!"

But little Ida was most amused at what the
student had said about her flowers, and she
thought about it for a long time. The flowers
drooped their heads because they were tired
out from dancing all night. No mistake about
it, they were ill. So she took them along to
her other playthings, which stood on a nice

little table where she kept all her treasures in a drawer. Her doll, Sophie, lay sleeping in her little bed, but Ida said to her: "You really must get up, Sophie, and be content with sleeping in the drawer to-night. The poor flowers are ill, and so they must sleep in your bed, then perhaps they will get well again."

She picked up the doll, which looked cross and never said a word, because it was annoyed at having to give up its bed.

Ida laid the flowers in the doll's bed, tucked them well up and told them to lie quite still while she made them some tea; then they would be well enough to get up next morning. She pulled the curtains close round the little bed, so that the sun shouldn't shine into their eyes.

66

All that evening she couldn't stop thinking about what the student had told her and, now that it was time to go to bed herself, she had first to take a peep behind the curtains drawn across the window, where her mother's beautiful flowers were standing. They were hyacinths and tulips, and she whispered to them quite softly: "I know perfectly well where you're going to-night!" But the flowers pretended they didn't understand a word, and they never stirred a leaf; but little Ida knew perfectly well what they were up to.

When she had got into bed, she lay for a long time thinking how jolly it would be to see the beautiful flowers dancing out there at the King's castle. "I wonder if my flowers really went too." But then she fell asleep. In the middle of the night she woke up again; she had been dreaming about the flowers and the student whom the Councillor scolded because he filled her head with rubbish. There wasn't a sound in the bedroom where Ida lay, the night-light was quietly burning on the table, and her father and mother were asleep.

"I wonder if my flowers are still lying in

Sophie's bed", she said to herself; "I *should* like to know!" She sat up in bed and looked over at the door, which stood ajar. In there lay the flowers and all her playthings. She listened carefully, and then it was just as though she heard a piano being played in the next room, but quite softly and more beautifully than she had ever heard before.

"That must be the flowers all dancing in there!" she said. "Oh dear, how I should like to see them!" But she didn't dare get up for fear of waking her father and mother. "If only they would come in here!" she said. But the flowers never came, and the music went on playing so beautifully that she couldn't stay where she was any longer, it was too lovely. She crept out of her little bed and went softly across to the door and peeped into the next room. Oh, it was really too amusing, what she saw in there.

There was no night-light of any sort, but all the same it wasn't a bit dark, for the moon was shining through the window on to the middle of the floor—it was almost as clear as daylight. All the hyacinths and tulips were standing on the floor in two long rows; there wasn't one left in the window, where the pots stood empty. Down on the floor all the flowers were dancing round so nicely together, actually doing the Grand Chain, and holding each other by their long green leaves as they swung round. But

over at the piano sat a tall yellow lily, which little Ida was sure she had seen last summer; for she remembered the student saying: "Isn't it like Miss Lena!" Everybody had laughed at him, but now Ida, too, thought that the long yellow flower really was like Miss Lena. It had just the same way of sitting at the piano, and

69

of turning it's sallow oval face first to one side
and then to the other, while it nodded time
to the pretty music. Nobody noticed little
Ida.

Next she saw a big blue crocus jump on to
the middle of the table, where her playthings

were lying, and go straight up to the doll's bed
and pull aside the curtains. There lay the sick
flowers; but they sat up at once and nodded to
the others that they would gladly come down
and join in the dancing. The old chimney-sweep,
whose lower lip had broken off, stood up and
bowed to the dainty flowers, which didn't look
in the least ill, but jumped down among the
others and enjoyed themselves like anything.

70

Suddenly something seemed to fall down off the table. Ida saw that it was the teaser she had been given for the carnival; it had jumped down, because it felt it was really one of the flowers. It certainly looked fine with its paper streamers, and at the top of it was a little

wax doll, wearing just such a wide-awake hat as the Councillor went about in. The teaser, on its three red wooden legs, hopped right in among the flowers and stamped away like anything, for it was dancing the mazurka, and that's a dance the other flowers couldn't manage, because they were too light to stamp properly.

All at once the wax doll at the end of the teaser seemed to grow bigger and taller; it

71

whirled round above its own paper flowers and shouted at the top of its voice: "What rubbish to put into a child's head! All stuff and non-sense!" The wax doll was the very image of the Councillor, all sallow and grumpy, in his wide-awake hat, but the teaser's paper flowers kept curling round his thin legs, and then he shrank together and became a little shrimp of a wax doll again. It was such fun to watch, and little Ida couldn't help laughing. The teaser went on dancing and the Councillor had to dance as well. It made no difference whether he grew large and lanky or remained the little yellow wax doll in the big black hat, he had to keep on dancing—till at last the other flowers, and especially those which had been lying in the doll's bed, begged him off, and the teaser stopped. At the same moment there was a loud knocking inside the drawer, where Ida's doll, Sophie, was lying among a lot of other playthings. The chimney-sweep ran along to the edge of the table and, lying full length on his stomach, he managed to work the drawer a little way open. Sophie sat up and looked around her in utter astonishment. "Why,

there's a dance going on here!" she said.
"Why didn't anyone tell me about it?"

"Will you dance with me?" said the chimney-sweep.

"I should think so! You're a fine one to dance with!"—and she turned her back on him. Then she sat down on the drawer, thinking that one of the flowers would be sure to come and ask her for a dance; but nobody came. She kept coughing—ahem! ahem!—it made no difference, not a soul came up to her. So the chimney-sweep danced by himself, and he didn't get on at all badly either.

And now, as none of the flowers seemed to notice Sophie, she let herself fall down, plump! on to the floor. It was a terrific thud. All the flowers came running up and stood round her, asking if she had hurt herself. They all behaved so nicely to her, especially the flowers who had been lying in her bed; but she hadn't hurt herself in the slightest, and all Ida's flowers said: "Thank you for the lovely bed" and made a great fuss of her and took her along to the moonlight in the middle of the floor and danced with her, while the other flowers made a ring round them. Sophie was delighted, and told them they were quite welcome to keep her bed, as she didn't a bit mind sleeping in the drawer.

But the flowers answered: "Thank you very, very much, but we can't live very long; we've only got till to-morrow. But please tell little Ida to bury us out in the garden where the canary was buried; then we shall sprout up again next summer and be far prettier."

"Oh, no! You mustn't die", said Sophie, as she kissed the flowers. At the same moment the drawing-room door opened, and a whole throng of beautiful flowers came dancing in. Ida couldn't make out where they came from, but of course they were all the flowers which had come in from the King's castle. Two lovely roses, wearing little crowns of gold, led the way; they were the King and Queen. Next came the most charming stocks and carnations, bowing in every direction. There was a band playing, too—great poppies and peonies blowing away on pea-shells till they were purple in the face, and harebells and little white snowdrops tinkling along as if they had real bells.

74

It was such funny music. After that came a lot of other flowers, and they all danced together—the blue violets and the red daisies, the ox-eyes and the lilies-of-the-valley. And it was pretty to see how the flowers all kissed each other. At last they said good-night to one another, and little Ida also crept away to bed, where she dreamt of all she had seen.

When she got up next morning, she went straight along to the little table, to see if the flowers were still there. She drew back the curtains of the little bed—yes, there they all lay together; but they were quite withered, much more than they were yesterday. Sophie was still in the drawer where Ida had put her; she was looking very sleepy.

"Do you remember what you were to tell me?" asked little Ida; but Sophie looked very stupid and didn't say a word.

"You're very naughty", said Ida, "and yet they all danced with you." Then she took a little cardboard box, which had a pretty design of birds on it, and taking off the lid she placed the dead flowers inside it. "There's a nice coffin for you", she said, "and later on, when my Norwegian cousins arrive, they will help me to bury you out in the garden, so that you can sprout up again next summer and become still prettier."

The Norwegian cousins were two lively boys called Jonas and Adolph, whose father had

just given them new bows and arrows, and they brought these with them to show to Ida. She told them all about the poor dead flowers, and they got leave to bury them. The two boys walked in front with the bows over their shoulders, and little Ida followed with the dead flowers in the pretty box. Out in the garden they dug a small grave. Ida first kissed the flowers, and then she placed them, box and all,

76

in the earth; and, as they hadn't any guns or cannons, Adolph and Jonas fired a salute over the grave with their bows and arrows.